Meet

Rosa Parks

Meet
Rosa Parks

By Patricia A. Pingry
Illustrated by Steven Walker

ideals children's books.
Nashville, Tennessee

ISBN -13: 978-0-8249-5578-6

Published by Ideals Children's Books
An imprint of Ideals Publications
A Guideposts Company
535 Metroplex Drive, Suite 250
Nashville, Tennessee 37211
www.idealsbooks.com

Library of Congress CIP data on file

Film separations by Precision Color Graphics, Franklin, Wisconsin

Printed and bound in Mexico

10 9 8 7 6 5 4 3 2 1

For Abbey —PAP

A special thanks to Evelyn —SW

I did not get on the bus to get arrested;

I got on the bus to go home. . . .

I had no idea that history was being made.

I was just tired of giving in.

—ROSA PARKS

Little Rosa Parks was walking home from school one day. A white boy on roller skates whizzed by and shoved her off the sidewalk. Rosa pushed him back.

"**Don't you push my son,**" a white woman yelled at Rosa. "**I can send you to jail for pushing a white boy!**"

"**He pushed me first!**" said Rosa. "**I wasn't bothering him, so he shouldn't push me.**"

But in the South, where Rosa lived, there were special laws, called Jim Crow laws, for African Americans. These laws kept black people and white people apart.

Black children could not go to school with white children. Black people could not drink from the same water fountains as white people. Black people could not even wait for a train in the same room as white people.

Rosa knew that was not fair. But it was the law.

Rosa was born February 4, 1913, in Tuskegee, Alabama.

She had a little brother. His name was Sylvester. Her mother,

Leona, taught school. Her father, James McCauley, built

houses. He was away most of the time looking for work.

The McCauleys worked hard, but they never had much money.

When Rosa was two years old, she moved with her mother and brother

to her grandparents' farm in Pine Level, Alabama.

Rosa loved to run through the woods on her grandfather's farm. She liked to play beside the streams. And she looked forward to Sundays at the A.M.E. church.

In Pine Level, Rosa and Sylvester walked to a one-room school that was only for black children. White children rode the bus to a big school. It was the law.

When Rosa was eleven years old, she went to to school in Montgomery. She studied sewing, cooking, and the Bible.

Rosa loved school, but when her grandmother became sick, Rosa had to go back home and take care of her. After her grandmother died, Rosa went back to Montgomery to school and to her first job as a seamstress.

But Rosa had to quit school once more and go back to Pine Level when her mother became ill. Her mother got well, but Rosa did not return to school then.

One day, Rosa met a young barber named Raymond Parks. Parks helped many African Americans. Rosa liked him, and she liked that he helped others. When Raymond asked Rosa to marry him, she said yes.

Rosa went back to school and earned her diploma. And she joined Raymond in helping the black people of Montgomery. They helped them when they were sick. They helped them when they were broke. They helped them when they were arrested.

Every day Rosa rode a bus to work. African Americans had to sit in the back of the bus. It was the law in Alabama.

In the middle of the bus were two special rows of seats. Black people could sit in these rows, but only if a white person didn't need to sit there.

Then the African Americans must give up their seats and move to the back. They could not even sit in the same row as a white person. It was the law.

When African Americans gave up their seats, they couldn't just walk to the back of the bus. Most of the time, they had to go out the front door and walk around to the back door.

Sometimes, the bus driver would take off before the black person could get back on the bus! Once, this happened to Rosa. It was humiliating. It was mean. It was wrong.

After work on December 1, 1955, Rosa waited in the dark for the Cleveland Avenue bus. When it arrived, she walked up the steps and sat down in the first seat available. Rosa was tired and wanted to go home. She might even listen to some Christmas carols on the radio.

Rosa was sitting in the first of the middle rows that were for blacks— if they were not needed for white people.

At the next stop, white people got on the bus. They took up all

the front rows. They filled up the seats in the row in front of Rosa.

Then more white people got on the bus.

The black women sitting
across the aisle from Rosa got up.

The black man sitting next to
Rosa got up. Rosa moved her legs
so he could pass.

Then Rosa slid over to his seat
and looked out the window.

The bus driver came back to Rosa. He told her she would have to get out of that seat. It was the law.

Rosa was tired of giving up her seat for white people. She was tired of being pushed around just because of the color of her skin.

So Rosa sat very still.

"Are you going to stand up?" the bus driver yelled.

"No," Rosa softly answered.

The bus driver said he would call the police.

"You may do that," Rosa said.

The police came. They took her to jail.

In Montgomery, there were many African Americans who wanted the bus law changed. They were all tired of being told where to sit on a bus.

So African Americans stopped riding the buses. Through the cold winter, they walked to work.

Through the rainy spring, they carpooled to grocery stores. And all through the hot summer, they walked. And they walked. And they walked.

Rosa went to court. The judge said she was guilty.

But the highest court in the land, the United States Supreme Court, said **no one could tell African Americans, or anybody else—where to sit on a bus!**

This was the new law.

On December 20, 1956, Rosa once again got on the Cleveland Avenue bus. She sat down in the front row.

Today in the United States, anybody can sit anywhere on any bus

because one woman politely but firmly refused to give up her seat.

It's the law.